Rounding Third

Zen. Baseball. Poems.

Paul Kocak

Kocak Wordsmiths Ink

ISBN-13: 978-0615750989
ISBN-10: 0615750982

Imprint logo:
leonard assante :: assante design inc.

Kocak Wordsmiths Ink
347 Whittier Avenue
Syracuse, NY 13204

To Raymond

Pregame Warm-up

I call this a book of zen baseball poetry, but don't let that scare you. You can enjoy this if you are neither a zen practitioner, nor a baseball fan, nor a poetry lover. How can I get away with saying that? I say that because I invite you to stop, look, and listen. We can all do that, can't we? I am inviting you, my reader, to read these words and picture moments of athletic grace, glee, or glory. You are invited to observe and celebrate moments of triumph, whether in ordinary daylight on emerald fields or under the glare of stadium lights.

Baseball and poetry are merely vehicles here for mindful reflection.

I make no claim that what you read here achieves greatness or perfection. My words are merely snapshots, part of a slide show of memories and emotion.

You will also see that my lens is idiosyncratic and selective, skewed toward my team, the San Francisco Giants. I can't help that. The heart has stubborn ways.

A word on my pricing: this book has fewer words than some of my other works and yet it may cost more. What's up with that? Well, we are not in the Charles Dickens era whereby writers get paid by voluminous word counts in weekly magazine installments. You might even say I am making a statement that the words in poetry count for more. The economy of brevity. Less is more. (Or you might simply accuse me of naked capitalism.) Plus, all that white space has a cost, too. Consider it the heavy silences between the words as in a Harold Pinter play.

Nevertheless, I hope you find this quirky assemblage of words rewarding. If even one part of one poem tugs at you in some heartfelt way, this modest collection has achieved its goal. For that I am grateful.

Paul Kocak

Syracuse, N.Y.

January 3, 2013

IN THE GAME

Rounding Third

I could do that

Tap my glove

Gallop hat's off

Horizon bound

Basket catch twirl homeward

I could do that

I all but said to the strangers

In the park

All shiny youth

On my sunset stroll

I could do that

If you only knew

In my dreams

Of Technicolor yesterday

Long gone

Rounding third

In Those Days

In those days

He wrapped his arms around me

Bracketing my hands on a bat

The swing ours

Hit or miss

In those days

I felt encircled

Firm as the sun

Sure as iron

Hot or cold

In those days

We knew neither past nor future

Neither fear nor fight

Just the pitch tossed to us

Frozen in time

Zen and the Art of Baseball Poetry

bases loaded

full count

two outs

zero

zero

this time

this field

these players

this pitch

this swing

this here

and

now

this

. . .

wow

ICONS AND OTHER PORTRAITS

dirt-caked cleats

bat tap

dig in right foot

hand twirls grip

one-armed swing

in the gap

hat flying

body sliding

home

free

Say Hey

Willie Mays

feet close

knees bent

eyes intent

batting majesty

power

grace

as constant as the Mississippi

Stan Musial

splendid splinter

stride of symmetry

smooth as silk

sultan of swing

Teddy Ballgame

fighter hero

Fenway immortal

American icon

Ted Williams

leg skyward

ball anchoring

slingshot trickery

magical mastery

Juan Marichal

samurai hurler

inscrutable slider

Lefty

king of the hill

and all its environs

win or lose

sensei

Steve Carlton

glowering and towering

warrior without fear

ball in hand

weapon or wand

fierce fireballer

general in charge

take no prisoners

Bob Gibson

basket catcher

spray hitter

missile-arm rocket man

Pirates' proudest leader

true hero beloved

by the lost and the found

he gave us his life

one moment at a time

Roberto Clemente

crisscrossed wrists

righted mightily

flash of power

forging home-run history

from Milwaukee to Atlanta

and everlastingly beyond

quiet strength

endurance

grace in action

Henry Aaron

wooden windmill

kinetic energy

revving rallies

Three Rivers symmetry

"We are family"

patriarchal powerhouse

Willie Stargell

mighty Stretch

44

ready for takeoff

deep down swoop

swinging for Saturn

gentle Giant

forever faithful

Willie McCovey

jack-rabbit speed

farmboy arms and wrists

switch-hitting

Oklahoma homer machine

the glory of the Yanks

Number 7

Mickey Mantle

the Bambino

Sultan of Swat

larger than life

in mink coats

smoking cigars

booze and broads

tiptoeing homeward

pointing to his destiny

American icon

the Babe

there is no other

Babe Ruth

from the plains

simple grace

unheralded still

path forger

record breaker

urban exile

61 in 61

Roger Maris

get it done

with power, speed, grit

in any league

a leader

Frank Robinson

in Jackie's shadow

too forgotten

Cleveland's pioneer

making history

with talent and verve

Larry Doby

Joltin' Joe

Marilyn Monroe

graveside roses

stoic heroics

56 games

son of a fisherman

brother outfielder

the Yankee clipper

sailing into history

Joe Dimaggio

oval grandeur

rusting

empty seats

long march home

"win the pennant!" faintly echoes

Polo Grounds

bye

FEAST OF CHAMPIONS, V. 2012

preacherman

evangelist of the heart

passion in every pore

spindly fire

praying mantis magic

Hunter Pence

winsome visage

earnest élan

sly smile

wicked slider

victory dance

etched eternal

Sergio Romo

from the ash heaps

of burnt millions

firebird rises

salvation's arc

at the brink

history rewritten

"Barry! Barry! Barry!"

brotherly warrior

Barry Zito

tough as nails

sure as iron

heart of soul

arms to the heavens

drinking in rain

elixir of the gods

iconic imprint

Marco Scutaro

how to spell "relief"

secret weapon

legend's locks

ready and able

liquid motion

avenging angel

Tim Lincecum

dugout antics

Tolstoy's beard

pulse of pride

eyes of ice

burning dance

"we hardly knew ye"

Brian Wilson

sweet swing

sweep tag

Fielder crusher

blue eyes

signal caller

twin father

game face

team dream

Buster Posey

bubblegum-chewer

fence-railing plunger

smile-inviter

Kung Fu Panda

three Ruthian bombs

seismic shift

rock the house

"Let Panda Eat!"

Pablo Sandoval

patrolling the meadows

saluting the foe

saluting fellow Giants

saluting us

king of triples

we salute you

Angel Pagan

dazzling shortstop

surprise tripler

Giants fan

dream come true

wearing a ring

Brandon Crawford

perfecto savior

flying acrobat

speedy scorer

White Shark

Gregor Blanco

flash of leather

quick hands

run stopper

sweet stroke

Baby Giraffe

Brandon Belt

mountain man

Southern boy

steady timber

hurler hero

Matt Cain

undertaker's visage

sheriff in town

don't mess

law and order

tossing strikeouts

MadBum

Madison Bumgarner

long night's journey

into day

this day

hashtag miracle

narrative arc

bull of victory

strong of heart

Ryan Vogelsong

mumbling on the mound

prayers and exhalations

mowing batters down

exhortations and exaltations

dragon slayer

Jeremy Affeldt

set-up or closer

give me the ball

fastball or slider

give me the ball

no matter who the batter

give me the ball

Santiago Casilla

sidearm sneaky

psychology maven

lefty specialist

subterranean magician

Javier Lopez

windmill waver

hand stopper

guitar hero

grateful alive

Tim Flannery

rounding third

tagging home

Game 4

winning run

madman thrill

raging score

riotous joy

Ryan Theriot

Cheshire smile

Buddha basking

sea captain

padre confessor

brother-in-arms

commander courage

ring-bearer

trophy-raiser

Bruce Bochy

Uncompromising Positions

cagey sage

coy chessman

regal rogue

winding up time

and space

blazing magic

risking life and limb

success and failure

on the wings of will

and desire

as they orbit

abandon

PITCHER

masked Buddha

receiver

giver

ying-yang game-reader

sensei

defender

CATCHER

balletic stretch

hawkish scoop

angular sentinel

cheetah bunt-charger

FIRST BASEMAN

race rightward

one-hop

snow-cone snag

lightning lash

out at first

SECOND BASEMAN

arc of night

poised to orbit

caughtus interruptus

stabbing the heavens

physics defeated

SHORTSTOP

knees bent

eyes locked

arms loose

pounce on the line

triple thwarted

run to dugout

THIRD BASEMAN

back back back

track track track

wait

wait

see

seize

leap

arm stretched to sinew

fans vying

horsehide

home to leather

web magic

still there

roars

LEFT FIELDER

meadow glistening

evening dew

nightstar soaring

over shoulder

gravity surrendering

coaxed by leather

and desire

out

CENTER FIELDER

cornered

nearly trapped

walled in

racing to oblivion

space

losing ground

time running out

neither fair nor foul

saved by the glove

RIGHT FIELDER

bouncing bullet to short

toss to dashing dancer

pirouettes

rocket to first

6-4-3 DOUBLE PLAY

SCENES

rippling flags / hitter harbingers / pitcher
pedantry

wind to center / racing fielder / wall eclipsed /
call me Homer

rocket from right / catch / sweep / tag / run
erased

lost in the lights / blinded by vision /
surrendering to the dark / hoping for purchase
/ however fleeting

catcher's cannon / runner's demise / dust rising

POSTGAME WRAP

The Fan's Lament

I would have waltzed

if I could

but for two left feet.

I would have stolen bases

left and right

if I could

but for loss of speed

and cunning.

I would have tossed shutouts

in my sleep

but for waking

to blistering bats

and blazing liners.

And I would have cranked homers

over every fence

in every yard

to cheering throngs

if I could

but for tiny wrists

and mortal eyes.

So I became a fan

and wrung my hands

and sold my soul

sometimes sailing high

most times treading water.

Along the way

I have met you

and you, me

to make it worth the while.

Coming Home

Past the waving arms

The caution of age

I round third

Heading come

All abandon

And coltish glee

I stretch forth

All gambling gambol

Eyes on the prize

Going for broke

Sink or swim

Slide or crash

Out or safe

Ready or not

Here I come

Coming home